MW01241060

Reconstructing the past

Puzzle of the lost community at Yellow Hill

For the Cause Productions
2699 Heidlersburg Road
Gettysburg, PA 17325

For the Cause Productions is donating a portion of the proceeds from sale of this booklet to restoration and preservation of local historic sites.

Learn more about local history and the effort to save the cemetery at www.gettysburghistories.com.

ISBN: 978-1-4196-6602-5 (paper)

Originally published as *Reconstructing the Past: Puzzle of a Lost Community*
©2005 Debra Sandoe McCauslin

To my father, Sereck James Sandoe (1936–2003)

It takes a new generation, a later generation, our generation to rescue and save that which we find important. Let us always remember to save our stories.

—HISTORIAN & FILMMAKER KEN BURNS

Contents

Illustrations

Photos by the author unless otherwise noted

Preface

I have lived within 10 miles of Yellow Hill all my life. That was where my father grew up, his "stomping grounds," and he often spoke of it fondly. As a child I spent lots of time on Yellow Hill, working in the orchards on my grandfather's farm on Clear Springs Road. In those days my maternal grandparents lived just north of Bendersville, and we visited them often. As we drove through the Quaker Valley from Biglerville to Bendersville, I sat in the back of my mother's station wagon and looked out at the big houses, houses that looked like mansions to me, wondering who built them and wishing I could see inside. *(For more information about the Quaker Valley Friends, see Appendix V.)*

Through my later involvement in local preservation efforts, I learned something about the Quakers who owned those grand homes and the African American community that settled near them on Yellow Hill. I wondered why no descendents of those early African American residents live there now. The Yellow Hill community seemed to thrive for a time, enjoying friendly relations with their surrounding neighbors during the 1800s and early 1900s. What happened?

As I worked through the available information, I discovered that a substantial African American community existed at Yellow Hill, that they contributed to the regional economy through their work in local fruit-growing and iron-making industries, that they established close relationships with the Friends living in the Quaker Valley, and that they were active in local operations of the Underground Railroad. I was surprised that this did not seem to be widely known and appreciated.

During the course of my research for this book I was surprised to learn that my great-great-grandfather, Henry P. Sandoe, owned land that bordered property once owned by Edward Mathews, an early resident of Yellow Hill and benefactor of the Yellow Hill church (later known as Fairmount A. M. E.—African Methodist Episcopal—Church) and cemetery.

Another surprise was a chance meeting with Alisha Wansel Sanders, great-great-granddaughter of Edward Mathews. I walked into the Adams County Historical Society (ACHS) one day and saw a young lady studying the Mathews burial records. When I asked whether she was interested in Edward Mathews, she smiled and said that she was, that she was a family member. Here was serendipity; thinking there were none to be found, I'd stumbled upon one of Edward and Annie's descendents. Alisha and I have continued to share information to better understand the story of the Yellow Hill community; several of the references included here were Alisha's discoveries.

Many people were generous with their time and help as I wrote this book. Heartfelt thanks to Larry Bolin, Elwood Christ, Rick Cullison, Tom Ford, Dr. Charles Glatfelter, Ann Griffith, Sherry Hammond, Jonathan Mahlbacher, Douglas Miller, Wayne Motts, Betty Myers, George Nagle, Karen Saltzgiver, Alisha Sanders, Raymond Schott, Patrice Smith, Timothy H. Smith, Sheryl Hollis Snyder, Arthur Weaner, and especially Rick McCauslin and Justin McCauslin. If I have omitted anyone, please forgive me.

For her help and encouragement I thank Betty Myers, who years ago advocated preservation of the Yellow Hill cemetery in a speech before the Adams County Historical Society. Her work at Gettysburg's Lincoln Cemetery inspired me. Becky Sachs, who lived on Yellow Hill, and Myrna Morton have also spoken out for preservation of the cemetery. I am indebted to them and to all those who have encouraged my interest in the site.

I hope you will enjoy learning about this "lost community" as I have, and that you will support the effort to preserve the Yellow Hill cemetery. *(To learn how you can help, see page 62.)* Please share these stories with others and help to keep the memory of the Yellow Hill community alive.

A note on terminology While in this book I generally use the term "African American" to describe nonwhite members of the Yellow Hill community, I retain the terms "colored," "black," and "mulatto" when referring to historical works in which those terms are used.

Debra Sandoe McCauslin

1
Lost society recalled

Mysteries and unanswered questions remain about the people who lived and worked on Yellow Hill. But the area's historic significance is slowly coming to light.

The area we now call Yellow Hill was identified on the 1858 G. M. Hopkins map as "Pine Hill." The 1872 Butler Township map also refers to "Pine Hill" and, directly below, has the notations "Colored Ch." identifying a church and "E. Mathews" identifying property owned by Edward Mathews. Yet today the road connecting Route 34 and Route 234 is not Pine Hill but Yellow Hill Road. How did this change come about?

1.1 *Detail of the 1872 Butler Township map (enhanced)*

The dictionary lists one meaning of the word "yellow" as "a person having yellow or light brown skin." Pine Hill may have come to be called "Yellow" Hill simply because it described the people who lived there. Possibly it was

100 DOLLARS REWARD.

RAN AWAY from the Subscriber, living in Georgetown, a NEGRO MAN, named JACK; or

JOHN POSEY

Said fellow eloped on the 29th of June last, and it is supposed, he has by some means procured a pass. John is rather of a dark yellow complexion, or nearly black, 21 years of age, 5 feet 9 or 10

1.2 *Ad from an 1817* Adams Centinel *showing that "yellow" was commonly used to describe darker skin color*

given the name in recognition of Edward Mathews and his family, early residents.

According to Robert Bloom's *History of Adams County,* African Americans first settled in Butler and Menallen Townships in the late 1700s.[1] Census data indicate they were there in 1800 *(Appendix I).* The population grew during the early and mid-1800s, and by the 1860s a sufficient number were living there for them to build a church. They buried their dead in the church cemetery during the 1870s, '80s, and '90s. Their Civil War veterans were buried here. Newspaper and diary accounts from the 1840s through the 1920s describe Negro camp meetings on Yellow Hill. With the help of their Quaker neighbors, the residents were helping others slip the bonds of slavery, as evidenced in the 1845 Kitty Payne kidnapping trial *(Appendix III).*

From information about the African American population compiled and summarized by Dr. Charles Glatfelter, former Executive Director of the Adams County Historical Society, from 1860 Adams County

---

1. Robert L. Bloom, *A History of Adams County, Pennsylvania, 1700–1990* (Gettysburg, PA: Adams County Historical Society, c1992), 177.

census records, we can see that, after Gettysburg and the surrounding Cumberland Township, the second largest number of African Americans in Adams County were concentrated in Butler and Menallen Townships. The Butler and Menallen Township line runs right across the top of Yellow Hill.

Although it is not often mentioned in historical accounts, Butler and Menallen Township residents were part of the county's agricultural and manufacturing economy. Census records indicate that some of the African Americans living north of Bendersville worked in the iron-making industry. Some made the charcoal required for iron-making; others worked at a nearby forge— probably Laurel Forge, just over the Adams County line in Cumberland County. One man was listed in the census as "Forgemen," another as "Woodchopper." Trees had to be cut, stacked, and burned slowly to make charcoal. Charcoal pits can still be seen on Yellow Hill.

Edward Mathews is listed in the 1850 Butler Township census as black, his wife Annie, mulatto; in the 1860 census both were listed as mulatto. Edward and Annie were born in Maryland, but 12 of their 13 children were born in Pennsylvania.

Unlike many African American men at the time, Edward Mathews was a property owner, having purchased 16 acres from John and Mary Knaus (Knouse) in 1842 for $350. Also named on the property deed was Francis Gant, a Maryland-born 81-year-old black male.

1.3 *Entries for Cyrus Griest (near top) and Samuel Mathews (bottom) in the 1860 Menallen Township census records*

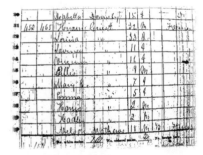

1.4 *Entries for Hiram Griest (near top) and Nelson Mathews (bottom) in the 1860 Menallen Township census records*

Documents show that two of Edward Mathews' sons lived on Quaker-owned fruit farms. Their occupations in census data were "Farmhand" and "Farm Laborer." The 1860 Menallen Township census lists the two boys, Samuel and Nelson, as black and living with Hiram and Cyrus Griest, Menallen Friends.

Census records show that African Americans living in Butler and Menallen Townships were not originally from the area. Larry Bolin and Karen Saltzgiver have compiled information about slaveholders[2] from county tax rolls. We know that slaves sometimes adopted their owner's surname, but comparisons of the

2. For more information about Adams County slaveholders, see *http://www.afrolumens.org*.

surnames of blacks or mulattos in the census to slave-holders' surnames from the tax rolls yielded no matches.

Some Yellow Hill residents lived in the area only briefly, some for many years. Records of marriages and births show that families were growing. Occupation listings tell us what residents did. Census data also show whether they owned property (and, if so, how much), whether they could read or write, where they were born, and whether they went to school. From newspaper accounts we know that they held Memorial Day services. The July 14, 1923 issue of the *Gettysburg Compiler* reported that the Yellow Hill Fire Company marched in the Fourth of July parade organized by the Adams County Fire-men's Association.

The Biglerville meeting was the occasion of a firemen's parade, base-ball game, festival, and dance.

The order of parade was as follows: The East Berlin Company with its band, led the line of march. Then followed Mt. Rock Centennial Company: McSherrystown, with its band; the Gettysburg Company with the new La France engine, and the Gettysburg Band; the Biglerville firemen and their apparatus in line and a band accompanied their ranks; Yellowhill Fire Company, composed of colored residents of Yellowhill, brought up the rear of the line.

Prizes awarded visiting fire companies for their showing in the parade went to the East Berlin company for having the highest percent-age of its membership in line. the

1.5 *The July 1923* Gettysburg Compiler *article may be the last newspaper reference to residents of the Yellow Hill community*

This article appears to be the last newspaper reference to the Yellow Hill community.

We are just beginning to understand the contributions of Yellow Hill residents to our past. Menallen Friends historian and Quaker Valley resident Posey Wright recalls her father-in-law's stories about "colored people" traveling up the hill over his family's land to church. Only remnants of this community remain today.

2
Freedom lies just north

Yellow Hill is located nine miles north of Gettysburg, site of the three-day battle that marked a turning point in the Civil War and the place Lincoln delivered the Gettysburg Address. Adams County rests on the Maryland border, right on the Mason-Dixon line separating slave states from free. For slaves escaping along the Underground Railroad, crossing the Mason-Dixon line meant a chance for freedom. Yellow Hill lies just about 20 miles north of that line.

Numerous "slave removals" occurred in Adams County in the early 1800s. Southern slaveowners wishing to reclaim a runaway slave in Pennsylvania first had to petition the court. Between 1827 and 1834, the Adams County court granted warrants to slaveowners from Virginia and Maryland for 12 such removals, indicating that runaway slaves were finding refuge in Adams County *(Appendix II)*.

In June of 1863, when the Confederate army crossed the Potomac and brought the war into the North, some of Gettysburg's African American residents fled to

Yellow Hill to avoid being captured and taken south to slavery.[3] Even before the war, however, the African American community of Yellow Hill had been helping others to freedom, and in this effort they were aided by sympathetic Quaker neighbors who shared the belief that all people should be free.

Yellow Hill is situated just above the Quaker Valley, where members of the Religious Society of Friends (or Quakers) first settled in the 1730s, meeting in their homes for decades thereafter. The Menallen Friends formed in 1780, and since 1830 have met at their current meetinghouse.[4] As they were throughout Pennsylvania, the Friends of the Quaker Valley were abolitionists. They testified along with some of the African American families on and around Yellow Hill at the 1845 trial of freed slave Kitty Payne who, with her three young children, was abducted from her home near Bendersville. The names of some of the Menallen Friends and their African American neighbors appear side by side on the Adams County Court's Quarter Session records listing witnesses who gave trial depositions supporting Payne's release[5] *(Appendix III)*.

---

3. Jean Odom of Gettysburg, PA, in an interview with the author, September 9, 2004.
4. Margaret B. Walmer, *Menallen Minutes, Marriages and Miscellany* (Bowie, MD: Heritage Books, Inc., 1992), 23.
5. Quarter Session Records (microfilm), 1846 (Gettysburg, PA: Adams County Courthouse).

According to local tradition and as reported in publications on the Underground Railroad, African American resident Edward Mathews[6] and Cyrus Griest[7], a Quaker Valley Friend, conducted others to freedom through the Underground Railroad. The location and proximity of their property holdings are noted on the 1858 G. M. Hopkins map of Adams County.

Was it a coincidence that these communities existed side by side, or did the African Americans deliberately settle near the Friends? Did the Friends help them to form the Yellow Hill settlement? Or, once neighbors, did they discover that they had similar interests and begin to work together to help escaping slaves to freedom? More questions than answers exist, although records continue to surface as the African American history of Yellow Hill and Butler and Menallen Townships is uncovered. We do know that the members of these communities enjoyed congenial working relationships.

6. Charles Blockson, *African Americans in Pennsylvania, Above Ground and Underground* (Harrisburg, PA: Sietz and Sietz, 2001), 188.

7. George M. Neely, Jr., "The Anti-Slavery Movement and Underground Railroad Activity in Adams County," Gettysburg College thesis, 1930 (Gettysburg, PA: Adams County Historical Society), 20.

3
Bringing others to the light

Locating documents proving that the Yellow Hill and Quaker Valley communities were part of the Underground Railroad is difficult. The Fugitive Slave Law of 1850 made it illegal to help slaves gain their freedom, and anyone caught aiding and abetting fugitive slaves was subject to heavy fines or imprisonment. Those who engaged in the practice kept quiet about it. Because of the secrecy surrounding this activity, little written evidence exists. But there is credible evidence to support the assumption that the Yellow Hill community and their Quaker Valley neighbors were part of the Underground Railroad.

The African American population of Adams County soared in the mid-1800s, before the outbreak of the Civil War. Most African Americans reported during the census that they were Pennsylvania-born; many older ones claimed Maryland and Virginia as their birthplaces, indicating that they had moved here from the south and during the days of slavery. The people of Yellow Hill and Quaker Valley were most likely doing their

3.1 *Gravestone of Cyrus Griest in the cemetery at the Menallen Friends Meetinghouse*

best to help runaway slaves. Quakers and African Americans often cooperated in this endeavor throughout Pennsylvania.

In his 1930 Gettysburg College thesis on the Underground Railroad in Adams County, student author George Neely noted that Adams County was situated just north of the Mason-Dixon line and that a number of Friends lived in Adams and York Counties[8]. Neely interviewed people who were aware of Underground Railroad activity on Yellow Hill, including A. W. Griest of Flora Dale. On

3.2 *Cyrus Griest home on Quaker Valley Road, Menallen Township*

Route 34 in the Quaker Valley, Flora Dale (called "Wrightsville" on older maps) is the home of the Menallen Meeting House. According to Griest, it was widely known that McAllister's Mill in Gettysburg was a stop on the Underground Railroad, and that the home of Cyrus Griest in the Quaker Valley between Pine (or Yellow) Hill and Rattlesnake Hill was another. He further reported that escaping slaves traveled the eight

8. Neely, 38.

miles from McAllister's Mill to the Quaker Valley on foot, and that upon arrival in Quaker Valley they were taken to Edward Mathews, who had founded a Negro settlement on Yellow Hill. In the middle of the night, Mathews took them to the home of Cyrus Griest and hid them in the springhouse. Mathews then tapped on Griest's bedroom window to let him know that he had guests. Later that morning, when the ladies awoke to make breakfast, food would be brought out to them.

3.3 *The Yellow Hill home of Edward and Annie Mathews house as it looks today*

Griest told Neely this happened about twice a month during the summer, but he never remembered it happening during the winter.

From the Cyrus Griest home fugitives could be conducted to York Springs, to the home of William and Phebe Wright (Griest relatives), or further north to Pine Grove Furnace in Cumberland County, just over the Adams County line, where a number of African Americans were employed. The iron master's house at Pine Grove Furnace was also reported to be an Underground Railroad station.[9]

9. John Alosi, *Shadow of Freedom: Slavery in Post-Revolutionary Cumberland County, 1780–1810* (Shippensburg, PA: Shippensburg University Press, 1994), 84.

3.4 *This painting of William Wierman Wright is displayed at the Adams County Historical Society.*

Neely's thesis also contains an interview with a man named Wright who named Edward Mathews, James McAllister, Adam Wert, Cyrus Griest, and William and Phebe Wright as members of an antislavery society.

One of the most relied-upon accounts of Underground Railroad activity is William Still's 1872 book, *The Underground Railroad,* in which the author claims that a thousand slaves were "aided to liberty" by William and Phebe Wright of York Springs. One of these fugitives was James W. C. Pennington. In his book, *The Fugitive Blacksmith,* Pennington refers to the Wrights as "WW" and "PW" and describes a six-month stay with them during which they taught him to read and write. He and the Wrights communicated for many years after his departure. Pennington later became a Presbyterian minister.

William and Phebe were related to many of the Wrights who settled in the Quaker Valley and gave their name to the town of Wrightsville (now called Flora Dale). Though Quakers usually refrain from participating in armed confict, William and Phebe's son, William

Wierman Wright, used engineering skills acquired at Gettysburg's Haupt Engineering School to assist General William T. Sherman during his famous March to the Sea. During that campaign, Wright served as Sherman's Chief Engineer *(Appendix VI)*.

4
Souls of everyday heroes

Among the individuals who made up the Yellow Hill community were **Edward** and **Annie Mathews,** citizens of Butler Township who were said to be active in the Underground Railroad. The parents of 13 children, 12

Pennsylvania born, Edward and Annie lived down a tree-shrouded lane in a house near the church lot on Yellow Hill. Edward died in 1874, Annie in 1893. Both are now interred at Lincoln Cemetery in Gettysburg, although Edward was first buried in the cemetery on Yellow Hill.[10]

4.1 *Annie and Edward Mathews are now buried in Lincoln Cemetery, located next to Gettysburg Hospital.*

Three of Edward and Annie's sons served in the U. S. Colored Troops, quite a contribution for one family. In 1864 son **William H. Mathews,** then about 14, ran away to join the army, hoping to serve with his older brothers Nelson, who had enlisted, and Samuel, who had been drafted. Military service was a

10. "Remains Reinterred," *Star and Sentinel* (Gettysburg, PA), May 20, 1903.

new opportunity for a black man. All three Mathews sons survived the war but paid a heavy price for the privilege of becoming soldiers.

Duties of soldiers in the U. S. Colored Troops were arduous. These soldiers received lower pay, less food, and poorer uniforms and equipment than the white soldiers. Many generals considered their colored troops expendable, of less value than their white troops. Colored soldiers were often ordered to build floating bridges over rivers to move the armies from shore to shore. This was very hazardous work as the men were out in the open and made easy targets. It was not uncommon for a colored soldier to drown after being shot in the leg. William Mathews was shot in the right knee. His pension records show that he also had pulmonary disease and could do no manual labor. He suffered for the rest of his life and died in 1891 from the injuries he sustained while serving in the U. S. Colored Troops.

4.2 Star and Sentinel *item announcing the death of William H. Mathews*

An announcement of William Mathews' death appeared in an 1891 issue of the *Star and Sentinel*:

It is with profound sadness that we chronicle the demise of

William H. Mathews of Gettysburg, but a former resident of this vicinity. The funeral was held on Sunday and the body was interred in the little grave yard by the church, situated in what is commonly known as Yellow Hill. It was our privilege to attend the funeral. The high esteem in which the deceased was held was proven by the large number of friends and acquaintances who gathered around the bier to pay their last tribute of respect to one whose character was unimpeachable and above that of the majority of ordinary men. Sunnyside[11], September 25.

Application for Burial of Deceased Soldier.

4.3 *Burial records indicate that William H. Mathews, a private in Company I of the 127TH, was buried in the graveyard next to Yellow Hill church. His body was later moved to Lincoln Cemetery.*

Lincoln Cemetery records indicate that William is now listed among the deceased at Lincoln Cemetery,[12] although his marker is not visible.

Mary Jane Mathews, William's wife, died in February 1890. At her death the Bendersville G. A. R. published this special resolution in a Gettysburg paper:

Resolutions passed by Serg't T. F. Elden Post, No. 507 G. A. R., of Bendersville, Pa., on the death of the wife of Comrade W. H. Matthews:
Whereas, it has pleased our heavenly Father, in his all-wise providence to remove from our midst,

---

11. Sunnyside, a small village near the Quaker Valley, later became known as Guernsey. The Quaker Run Road joins the Meetinghouse to Guernsey, through which the Gettysburg Harrisburg Railroad once transported passengers and freight.
12. Betty Dorsey Myers, *Segregation in Death: Gettysburg's Lincoln Cemetery* (Gettysburg, PA: Lincoln Cemetery Project), 69.

by the hand of death, the wife of our comrade W. H. Matthews,

Resolved, That we submit humble to the will of Divine Providence, recognizing His infinite power, and knowingly that all things that He doeth are for our good,

Resolved, That we greatly sympathize with our comrade and family in this their time of sorrow and grief,

Resolved, we hope our comrade will look forward to the time which is coming when they shall all be again united,

Resolved, That a copy of these resolutions be placed on file, a copy send to the bereaved family, and a copy sent to county papers for publication.

D. E. Taylor, W. P. Becker, S.E. Wampler
Committee

4.4 *Mary Jane Mathews' stone at Gettysburg's Lincoln cemetery. She may have once been buried at Yellow Hill.*

Mary Jane Mathews was likely buried at Yellow Hill cemetery and later relocated to Lincoln Cemetery, although no records have been found that confirm this.

The deaths of William and Mary Jane Mathews orphaned their children. The youngest, **Jessie Ellen Mathews,** was six. According to Adams County Orphan's Court records, Jessie was shuffled from one member of the family to another. Although her guardian never took Jessie into his home, he did secure a pension for her based on William's army service. However, Jessie never received any of the funds that were supposed to be placed in trust for her until she reached the age of 18.

Jessie was once harshly beaten by an aunt for failing to unravel tangled yarn. She had been ordered to untangle fours skeins of yarn and to rewind the yarn onto balls. She finished three of them but hid the fourth because it was too tangled. When her aunt discovered that she had hidden the last one, she beat Jessie, dragged her from the house, and threw her into the street where she was left to fend for herself, her body covered with welts.

After this episode Jessie went to live with a brother in Harrisburg. There she attended Harrisburg High School, graduating in 1904. She spent the next year teaching kindergarten.

In Pittsburgh Jessie met handsome law student Robert Lee Vann, and they married after he passed the bar. Vann started a law firm and later became involved with the *Pittsburgh Courier,* which became the number one Negro newspaper in the nation. His law cases were well documented in the *Courier,* helping him become a respected attorney. Vann later served as editor of the newspaper, and he served briefly in Washington during Franklin Roosevelt's presidency. In his speeches and in his editorials for the *Courier,* he always advocated the betterment of African Americans. Both Robert and Jessie served on national committees and boards. On the occasion of Robert's death in 1940, Jessie received flowers and telegrams from Joe Louis, Ella Fitzgerald, the Ink Spots, and Count Basie. She took over as president of the *Courier*, serving in the post until 1963. Jessie Mathews Vann died in 1967.

In October 1953 the popular television show "This Is Your Life," hosted by Ralph Edwards, featured the rags-to-riches story of this Yellow Hill orphan[13] who, through education, her determination to succeed, and the good works she undertook with her husband, had a productive and happy life.

4.5 *Headstones of Nelson and Hannah Mathews at Lincoln Cemetery. The G. A. R. marker (lower left) signifies that Nelson was a veteran, having served with the U. S. Colored Troops.*

Nelson Mathews, another son of Edward and Annie, was married to **Hannah,** the abusive aunt who had beaten young Jessie Mathews and turned her into the street, predicting that she "wouldn't amount to nothing." Jessie's 1967 obituary cited this incident, adding that her aunt was not only cruel but also a

13. Andrew Bunie, *Robert L. Vann of the* Pittsburgh Courier: *Politics and Black Journalism* (Pittsburgh, PA: University of Pittsburgh Press, 1974), 398.

bad prophet. Nelson and Hannah Mathews are buried in Lincoln Cemetery.

4.6 *Cora Mathews, daughter of William and Mary Jane Mathews, was probably first buried at Yellow Hill and then later moved to Lincoln Cemetery.*

Cora B. Mathews was a daughter of William and Mary Jane Mathews. Both Cora and Mary Jane died before William. Like William, Cora was likely buried in Yellow Hill cemetery and later relocated to Lincoln Cemetery, although no documents have been found to substantiate this.

Charles Parker, a soldier in the U. S. Colored Troops, married Sarah Butler, daughter of Peter Butler of Menallen Township, in 1867. According

4.7 *Charles Parker's remains were removed from the abandoned Yellow Hill cemetery and reinterred at Soldier's National Cemetery in 1936.*

to pension records in the National Archives, Parker suffered a gunshot wound to his right leg during the Battle of Gainesville (Florida). Records also show that after he left the army he coughed persistently and complained of weakness. Parker contracted typhoid pneumonia in the service, was sick within seven months of enlisting, and never was well after discharge. He died in 1877 at age 29, as a result of his service-related injuries. He must have joined the army

4.8 *National Park Service letter confirming
disinterment of Charles Parker's remains*

when he was about 16. Parker's pension files indicate that Sarah lived in Arendtsville and, later, on Gas Alley Avenue in York, and that she was very poor, almost starving. At the time of Parker's death, they had three children.

In a letter to Dr. Henry Stewart (son of Sallie Myers of Gettysburg), who was attempting to document veterans buried in Adams County cemeteries, the National Park Service acknowledged disinterment of Charles Parker's remains, stating that the body was in their vault. A 1936 newspaper story reporting the relocation of Parker's remains to the Soldier's National Cemetery in Gettysburg stated that "[H]e was interred from the now abandoned cemetery at Yellow Hill," indicating that the cemetery has been abandoned at least since the 1930s.

Basil Biggs, mulatto according to census records, was a veterinarian who lived in Gettysburg on one of the McPherson farms. Biggs' wife, Mary Jackson, was believed to be the sister of Edward Mathews.[14] His

---

14. Rogers T. Smith of Gettysburg, PA, in a 2004 interview with the author. His wife, Jessie Wansel Smith, a great-great-granddaughter of Edward Mathews, is named for Jessie Mathews Vann.

21

4.9 *Gettysburg veterinarian Basil Biggs was active in the Underground Railroad.*

4.10 *A portion of Basil Biggs' obituary*

obituary in the June 11, 1906, edition of the *Compiler* read in part:

> He was an active agent in the Underground Railroad and he took fugitives to the home of Edward Mathews in the Quaker Valley and the conduct of liberty was accomplished by the Quakers there . . . .. He was raised on a Quaker settlement near the Shepherd farm in Carroll County Maryland.

Raised on a Quaker settlement, Biggs was no doubt influenced by their abolitionist beliefs.

Aaron Mears worked at Laurel Forge (now part of Pine Grove Furnace State Park). In November 1879, while digging iron ore, he was fatally injured in a work-related accident. Age 21, Aaron was the only son of Benjamin Mears (sometimes Mars or Marse), who had settled in Menallen Township in the early 1800s and owned property north of Bendersville, near that owned by Peter Butler. A member of the Mears family later married a member of the Mathews family.

4.11 *Aaron Mears died in 1879 of injuries sustained on his job at Laurel Forge.*

African American residents labored on Adams County fruit farms, in the iron industry, and in other vocations for much of the nineteenth century. They helped these industries succeed before and after the Civil War. During the war they contributed their service, and many surviving veterans experienced prolonged suffering and early death as a result of their injuries.

Although some disinterments from the Yellow Hill cemetery have taken place, we have no evidence that all bodies have been moved. In a 1937 Gettysburg newspaper article, the York County Historical Society requested information on various graveyards, including the Yellow Hill cemetery. Recent information from York County indicates that in 1937 the only visible gravestones at Yellow Hill were those of John and Charlotte Naylor, who died in 1887 and 1888. Both gravestones were still there in the 1990s, and no records have been found to indicate that the Naylors were disinterred. When Charlotte Naylor's stone was removed for fear of vandals and placed in the care of the Adams County Historical Society, it was the only stone remaining in the cemetery.

The abandoned church lot and cemetery are sadly inadequate reminders of the contributions made to the history of Adams County over many decades by the Yellow Hill community.

5
A place of their own

In the 1800s an African American community already existed on Yellow Hill. How it came to be there we aren't sure. Residents may have settled there as freed citizens or as fugitive slaves who didn't want to run any farther. One thing we do know is that there were enough people of color living and working in the vicinity of Yellow Hill that they required a church and cemetery of their own. Though the people in this community lived freely, they could neither attend the white folks' church nor bury their loved ones in the same cemetery.

They choose lovely ground for the church lot. On a clear day, the view of Gettysburg from the Yellow Hill cemetery is spectacular. From this serene place, high atop Yellow Hill looking south, the town of Gettysburg and northern Maryland are spread out before you. How many runaway slaves stood in this spot and gazed into the southern distance, considering the life they had left behind?

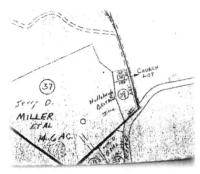

5.1 *Sixteen acres identified as the Miller property once belonged to Edward Mathews, who gave part of his land for a church lot.*

Edward Mathews owned 16 acres of land on Yellow Hill. He later gave part of this land for a church lot. In his 1874 will he says:

I give, devise and bequeath the ground where the Union church has been built, the land for church and yard around the church . . . to my beloved wife, Annie.[15]

While a "colored church lot" on Yellow Hill is noted on neighboring deeds, the land is currently unowned, untaxed, and landlocked. According to Adams County courthouse records, the plot plan identifies the "church lot" as lot #38. On the occasion of its consecration in 1869, the *Star and Sentinel* identified the church as "Yellow Hill Church," but later editions of the paper refer to it as Fairmount A. M. E. Church. On June 16, 1871, the *Star and Sentinel* mentioned that Rev. Charles Maddix had been named to serve St. Paul's A. M. E. Church in Gettysburg and the church at Yellow Hill *(Appendix IV)*.

5.2 *Announcement of church consecration in the August 1869* Star and Sentinel

15. Edward Mathews' will. (Gettysburg, PA: Adams County Court, 1874), file #4968. *Courtesy of Doug Miller.*

Before he died Mathews gave his daughter Martha a one-acre tract in front of the church, abutting Yellow Hill Road. When Annie sold her remaining 14 acres, ownership of the church lot was not transferred.

Yellow Hill was once a place where people of all ages, all colors, and all denominations worshipped together at evangelical camp meetings in late August of each year. In 1843 Menallen Friend William Wilson wrote in his personal diary that he attended such meetings,[16] suggesting that friendly relations existed between the Yellow Hill community and the Quaker Valley Friends. Evangelical and ecumenical camp (or woods) meetings sponsored by colored churches were a typical activity at the time. Circuit riding preachers roused attendees with stirring oratories and testimonies. Camp meetings, sometimes lasting for days, were usually held at the end of the summer.

stops.
THE woods meeting held by the colored people at "Yellow Hill" was largely attended on Sunday.

5.3 *Yellow Hill meetings occurred in the 1870s, as noted in the September 15, 1877* Compiler *(Gettysburg, PA).*

Who still rests in the cemetery at Yellow Hill? We know of John Naylor, buried in 1887, and Charlotte Naylor, buried in 1888. One headstone bore the initials "C. M. and L. N." The remains of some war veterans

---

16. William B. Wilson, *Diary of William B. Wilson, 1829–1871*, Vol. 2, *January 1838–December 1854* (Harrisburg, PA: State Library of Pennsylvania; from photostats in the possession of Dr. Albert Cook Myers), August 26 and 27, 1843.

originally buried there have been disinterred. Charles Parker was reinterred in the Soldier's National Cemetery, William Mathews in Lincoln Cemetery. The fact that some remains were removed does little to diminish the cemetery's significance; the fact that it was the original resting place makes Yellow Hill cemetery a historic site.

According to local folklore, the Yellow Hill church was deliberately burned down, although no primary source has been found to subtantiate the rumor. A gravestone removed from the cemetery in the 1990s and given to the Adams County Historical Society for safe-keeping bears a burial date of 1888, so it is likely the church burned down during the late 1880s or early 1890s. If deliberate arson, the burning may have been the result of animosity between some area families.

In an interview recorded at the Adams County Historical Society in 1986, Becky Sachs, whose family had lived on Yellow Hill since 1911, said she had been told that there was a pretty little church up there at one time, with a bell, a beautiful white picket fence, and a cemetery—a cemetery for colored folks. She remembered seeing pieces of the fence and the cornerstones of the church, which she thought measured about 20″ by 30′. She said the church had been burned deliberately but declined to mention the names of those rumored to be responsible for fear of embarrassing descendents still living in the area.

We may never discover who burned the Yellow Hill church, or even whether the fire was accidental or intentional. But those interested in local history are working to reconstruct and share with others the stories of the Yellow Hill community. And what better place to do this than right where their history was made, right at the heart of Yellow Hill. By preserving Yellow Hill cemetery, we can help to insure that this important piece of Adams County history is remembered.

6
Saving the past

Today a derelict cemetery, abandoned for nearly a century, and the Edward Mathews home are the only reminders of a community that once existed on Yellow Hill. For more than 35 years Dewey Bower, a member of the Biglerville American Legion, has remembered the

Yellow Hill community by placing an American flag in honor of the veterans buried in the cemetery. His actions have focused local attention on the area, and now the origins of the cemetery, its founders, and the congregation of the Yellow Hill church are being investigated with interest.

6.1 *Headstone of John Naylor. The original caption to this historic Philip Tyson photo reads, "These graves stones on Yellow Hill, three miles northwest of Biglerville, are the only remains of a settlement of negroes. Once slaves who sought refuge in the 'underground railroad' stations near here, they remained long after the war and eventually moved away to better opportunity."*

In 2003 John Phillips, attorney for the Historic Preservation Society of Gettysburg and Adams County (HPSGAC), completed a title search and determined that the church lot was, indeed, once part of Edward Mathews' 16 acres. The church lot measures 120′ by 80′ by 140′ by 90′, and its corners are clearly marked with stakes. Hollabaugh Brothers,

6.2 *We get a closer look at John Naylor's headstone in this photo taken by Myrna Morton, longtime advocate for preservation of Yellow Hill cemetery. According to locals, this stone was visible 20 or 30 years ago. Its current location is unknown.*

Inc., owns the property adjoining three sides of the church lot; the Miller property (formerly owned by Mathews) borders the fourth.

We don't know how many graves are in the church cemetery today. Though we know that John and Charlotte Naylor are still interred there, we don't know how many people were originally buried there. According to some older citizens, 20 to 30 stones were once visible. The only documented removal was that of Charles Parker, although a 1905 Gettysburg newspaper reported that Edward Mathews was moved. William Mathews, wife Mary Jane, and daughter Cora were probably moved; records indicate that they are now interred at Lincoln Cemetery.

6.3 *Timothy H. Smith holds the stone of Charlotte Naylor, who died in 1888. When this stone was given to the Adams County Historical Society in the 1990s, it was said to be the only stone remaining in the Yellow Hill cemetery.*

Bases that once held gravestones are visible in the church cemetery, but no headstones stand on them. Most have been vandalized or removed, but some, or parts, of them may lie just under the ground. The area was wooded for many years; leaves and erosion may have buried them.

6.4 *Headstone bases are visible in the church cemetery. All headstones have been vandalized or removed.*

We can learn more by subjecting the cemetery to ground-penetrating radar, which would detect the graves and the cornerstones of the church. Somewhere on that lot stood a church, and the footers to the church could be located; somewhere within the boundaries of the church lot was a cemetery, though its exact size and location are unknown. Objects or artifacts hidden beneath the ground may provide clues to what took place on the property.

We do know that the people of color who once lived there have moved away from Butler and Menallen Townships, most gone by 1900. Some Mathews descendents still live in Adams County and are interested in restoring Yellow Hill cemetery. Through a grass roots community effort with the HPSGAC, Yellow Hill cemetery may be preserved so that these stories can be told at that place where the Yellow Hill community had their own church, where they laid to rest their loved ones—some of them war heroes—high on beautiful Yellow Hill.

Currently, a visit to this site is technically illegal. Though township laws state that cemeteries must be open to the public, Yellow Hill cemetery is accessible only by crossing private property. The road on the east side of the church lot that once provided access to the cemetery no longer exists. A lane several feet wide was created on

the west side of the church lot, and another lane was created on the northern border to provide access to privately owned lots located behind the church lot. The HPSGAC is trying to negotiate an access agreement so that the cemetery, once accessible, can be maintained, restored, and preserved.

6.5 *The cemetery as it looked before trees were removed. The cemetery lot is beyond the large bins just visible through the trees.*

The community has already made an effort to clear the site and ready the land for restoration. Volunteers have supported this effort because they live nearby or are interested in the history of Yellow Hill. Some took part because they grew up there; others simply believed it

was the right thing to do.

In recent years Hollabaugh Brothers, Inc., has mowed and maintained the site, and removed debris from the church lot and adjoining property. Volunteers have removed trees and bramble from the cemetery area. Bertram Herbert, archaeologist and

6.6 *This base, which once held a headstone, was uncovered during tree removal. How many others lie just beneath the ground?*

6.7 *Dewey Bower of the Biglerville American Legion watches Butler Township crew remove a tree.*

6.8 *The site as it looked after tree removal. The remaining tree marks the supposed corner of the property.*

6.9 *The Biglerville 4-H planted ground cover on the cemetery lot to help keep the weeds from reestablishing themselves.*

cultural research specialist for the National Park Service at Gettysburg, supervised tree removal, during which care was taken to not uproot trees or disturb the soil since this would skew the results of ground-penetrating radar. With the ability to detect past underground activity, ground-penetrating radar can reveal whether and how much the earth has been disturbed below the surface.

The successful restoration of Gettysburg's Lincoln Cemetery provides an example of what can be done at Yellow Hill. A cooperative grassroots effort to preserve the cemetery would be a big step toward public recognition of the Yellow Hill community. If site access and other issues can be resolved, tours could be conducted to the site in order to tell the story of those who once lived here. School groups could visit the site and hear educational programs about slavery, freedom, diversity, and abolitionist activity. Also worth mentioning are contributions of the Mathews family and the African American community as a whole, how they worked with the Quakers, and what they accomplished.

We cannot alter past ignorance, but we can resolve not to repeat it. Preserving the cemetery on Yellow Hill is the right thing to do so that future generations will know the history of the people who lived there. Preserving the cemetery will permit us to tell their story at the very place where that history was made.

Let us act now to save Yellow Hill. *(To learn how you can help, see page 62.)*

Appendix

Census data on blacks, coloreds, and mulattos in Butler and Menallen townships, by year

TWP M/B	LAST NAME	FIRST NAME	AGE	VALUE OF PROPERTY	OCCUPATION	GENDER M/F	COLOR B/C/M	BIRTH-PLACE	COMMENTS
1800	*Total 1*								
M	Butler	Samuel							
1810	*Total 1*								
M	Morton	Jesse							
1820	*Total 13*								
M	Balm	William		2 living w/him			free C		
M	Marrs	Benjamin		2 living w/him			free C		
M	Anderson	Edward		2 living w/him			free C		
M	Buck	Jacob		1 living w/him					
M	Buck	Rosanah							
M	Linganore	Ester							
1830	*Total 33*								
M	Buck	Jacob		4 living w/him			free C		
M	Buck	Rosanna		6 living w/her			free C		
M	Lingamore	Ester					free C		
M	Lowers	Paul		11 living w/him					
M	Marrs	Benjamin		7 living w/him			free C		
1840	*Total 56*								
M	Anderson	Lydia		3 living w/her			C		
M	Barrens	Wm.		5 living w/him			C		
M	Buckmaster	Mich.		7 living w/him			C		
M	Jones	Amon		3 living w/him			C		
M	Laird	Robert		6 living w/him			C		
M	Marrs	Thomas		4 living w/him			C		
M	Marrs	Benjamin		5 living w/him			C		
M	Mathews	Edward		6 living w/him			C		
M	White	Daniel		1 living w/him			C		

TWP M/B	LAST NAME	FIRST NAME	AGE	VALUE OF PROPERTY	OCCUPATION	GENDER M/F	COLOR B/C/M	BIRTH-PLACE	COMMENTS
1840 continued		*Total 56*							
M	Woods	Isaac			6 living w/him		C		
1850		*Total 95*							
M	Anderson	Jesse	40		Laborer	M	B	PA	Living w/Peter & Harriet Butler.
M	Anderson	Lydia	70			F	B	MD	Living w/Daniel White.
B	Barks	Margarett	14			F	M	PA	Lived w/Benjamin & Jane Roberts family.
B	Black	Robert	14			M	M	Adams Co PA	Lived w/George & Barbara Weaver family, property $4,000.
M	Boyd	Abby I.	12			F	M	PA	Living w/Joel Fisher.
M	Brown	Thomas	75			M	B	MD	
M	Brown	David	9			M	M	PA	
B	Buck	Isaac	14			M	B	Adams Co PA	Lived w/Margarett, age 60, & Sarah Trone, age 31.
M	Buckmaster	Jacob	50	$300	Laborer	M	B	PA	
M	Buckmaster	Belinda	52			F	B	PA	
M	Buckmaster	George	22		Laborer	M	B	PA	
M	Buckmaster	Belinda	8			F	B	PA	
M	Buckmaster	Jane	6			F	B	PA	
M	Buckmaster	Philip	1			M	B	PA	
M	Buckmaster	Charles	1			M	B	PA	
M	Buckmaster	Stephen	11			M	B	PA	
M	Buckmaster	Michael	18		Laborer	M	B	PA	
M	Butler	Peter	33	$600	Laborer	M	M	MD	
M	Butler	Harriet	27			F	M	PA	
M	Butler	Sarah	6			F	M	PA	
M	Butler	Hannah	3			F	M	PA	
M	Butler	Samuel	1			M	M	PA	
M	Devonshire	John	21		Laborer	M	M	PA	Living w/Peter & Harriet Butler.
B	Gant	Francis	81			M	B	MD	Lived w/Edward & Ann Mathews family.
M	Green	James	45	$50	Laborer	M	B	VA	

TWP M/B	LAST NAME	FIRST NAME	AGE	VALUE OF PROPERTY	OCCUPATION	GENDER M/F	COLOR B/C/M	BIRTH-PLACE	COMMENTS
1850 continued		*Total 95*							
M	Green	Esther	47			F	B	PA	
M	Harrison	William	9			M	B	PA	Lived w/James & Vilet Sanders family.
M	Jones	Amos	50	$150	Laborer	M	M	MD	
M	Jones	Rachel	60			F	M	PA	
M	Mares	Benjamin Jr.	40	$250	Laborer	M	M	MD	Living w/Peter & Harriet Butler.
M	Mares	Leah	25			F	M	PA	Living w/Peter & Harriet Butler.
M	Mares	Elizabeth	6			F	M	PA	Living w/Peter & Harriet Butler.
M	Mares	Susan	3			F	M	PA	Living w/Peter & Harriet Butler.
M	Mares	Benjamin	73	$700	Laborer	M	M	MD	
M	Mares	Catherine	54			F	M	PA	
M	Mares	Eliza	22			F	M	PA	
M	Mares	Rachel	19			F	M	PA	
M	Mares	Sarah	16			F	M	PA	
M	Mares	Harriet	10			F	M	PA	
M	Mares	Samuel	6			M	M	PA	
M	Mares	Emma	3			F	M	PA	
B	Mathews	Edward	39	$350	Laborer	M	B	MD	
B	Mathews	Ann	29			F	M	MD	
B	Mathews	Samuel	11			M	B	MD	
B	Mathews	Nelson	9			M	M	PA	
B	Mathews	Nancy	6			F	M	PA	
B	Mathews	Jane	4			F	M	PA	
B	Mathews	Wm.	2			M	M	PA	
B	Mathews	Edward	1			M	M	PA	
M	Michaels	Susan	45			F	B	PA	
M	Michaels	Sally	25			F	B	PA	
M	Michaels	Mary	18			F	B	PA	
M	Michaels	Henrietta	14			F	B	PA	
M	Michaels	Joseph	16		Laborer	M	B	PA	
M	Michaels	Henry	9			M	B	PA	

TWP M/B	LAST NAME	FIRST NAME	AGE	VALUE OF PROPERTY	OCCUPATION	GENDER M/F	COLOR B/C/M	BIRTH-PLACE	COMMENTS
1850 continued		*Total 95*							
M	Michails	James	51	$150	Laborer	M	B	PA	
M	Michails	Susan	50			F	B	PA	
M	Michails	Maria	18			F	B	PA	
M	Michails	Joseph	12			M	B	PA	
M	Pain	Mary	10			F	M	PA	Living w/John Wright, farmer, age 68, property value, 3500, PA.
M	Plowden	Jane	14			F	B	PA	Living w/Daniel & Lydia Peters .
M	Plowden	Peter	50			M	B	VA	
M	Plowden	Mary	10			F	B	PA	
M	Plowden	Ammond	7			M	B	PA	
M	Plowden	Cathrine	3			F	B	PA	
M	Plowden	William	1			M	B	PA	
M	Plowden	Nancy	35			F	B	PA	
*B	Roberts	Benjamin	59		Laborer	M	B	VA	Illiterate
B	Roberts	Jane	29			F	B	VA	Illiterate
B	Roberts	Eliza	10 mo			F	B	PA	
B	Roberts	Edward	6			M	B	PA	
B	Roberts	Howard	3			M	B	PA	
*B	Robinson	Benjamin	55		Laborer	M	B	VA	
B	Robinson	Jane	25			F	B	VA	
B	Robinson	John	14		student	M	B	PA	
B	Robinson	Margarete	16		student	F	M	PA	
B	Robinson	Edward	6			M	B	PA	
B	Robinson	Howard	3			M	B	PA	
B	Robinson	Infant	1			F	B	PA	
M	Sanders	James	65	$100		M	B	PA	Blind
M	Sanders	Vilet	65			F	B	PA	
M	Sanders	Richard	21		Laborer	M	B	PA	
M	Sanders	Joshua	16		Laborer	M	B	PA	
M	Sanders	Charita	14			F	B	PA	

*Possible duplicate entry

TWP M/B	LAST NAME	FIRST NAME	AGE	VALUE OF PROPERTY	OCCUPATION	GENDER M/F	COLOR B/C/M	BIRTH-PLACE	COMMENTS
1850 continued		*Total 95*							
M	White	Daniel	69			M	B	VA	
M	White	Fanny	32			F	B	PA	
M	White	Elyah	15			M	B	PA	
M	White	John	9			M	B	PA	
M	White	Jacob	1			M	B	PA	
M	Wilson	Peter	48		Laborer	M	M	PA	
M	Wilson	Cathrine	53			F		PA	
M	Wilson	Louisa	7			F	M	PA	
M	Woods	John	22		Laborer	M	B	PA	
M	Woods	Rachel	18			F	B	PA	
M	Woods	Infant	3 mo			F	B	PA	
1860		*Total 76*							
M	Biggins	George	15		Woodchopper	F	B	PA	Gender said F but probably M. Attended school.
M	Buckmaster	Jacob	45	real $1000, personal $70		M	B	PA	Illiterate
M	Buckmaster	Reachel	45			F	B	PA	Illiterate
B	Butler	Jesse	68		Farmhand	M	B	PA	Lived with Jacob Listle. Illiterate.
M	Butler	Peter	43	real $1200, personal $250	Forgeman	M	B	PA	
M	Butler	Harriet	38			F	B	PA	
M	Butler	Hannah	13			F	B	PA	Attended school.
M	Butler	Henry	7			M	B	PA	Attended school.
M	Butler	Samuel	11			M	B	PA	Attended school.
M	Butler	Harriet	5			F	B	PA	
M	Butler	Thomas	1			M	B	PA	
M	Butler	Thomas	38		Forgeman	M	B	PA	
M	Coleman	Nathan	65	real $350, personal $30	Day laborer	M	B	VA	
M	Coleman	Nancy	65			F	B	PA	Illiterate
M	Coleman	William	11			M	B	PA	Illiterate
M	Coleman	Elizabeth	10			F	B	PA	
M	Coleman	John	6			M	B	PA	

TWP M/B	LAST NAME	FIRST NAME	AGE	VALUE OF PROPERTY	OCCUPATION	GENDER M/F	COLOR B/C/M	BIRTH-PLACE	COMMENTS
1860 continued		Total 76							
M	Coleman	Samuel	2 mo			M	B	PA	
M	Devinger	John	36		Day Laborer	M	M	PA	Lived w/Mars family.
M	Gooden	Levan	3			F	M	PA	Lived w/Susan Michaels.
M	Goodwin	Sarah	7			F	B	PA	Lived w/Susan Michaels.
B	Harr	John	44	real $1000, personal $500	Day laborer	M	M	PA	
B	Harr	Rachel	40			F	M	PA	
B	Harr	John	8			M	M	PA	Attended school.
B	Harr	Wilson	4			M	M	PA	
B	Harr	Charles	2			M	M	PA	
M	Harris	Fanny	40		Domestic	F	B	PA	
M	Harris	Elizabeth	18		Domestic	F	B	PA	
M	Harris	Mary	10			F	B	PA	
M	Jones	Amon	56	real $200, personal $80	Day laborer	M	M	MD	Illiterate
M	Jones	Rachel	49			F	B	PA	
M	Mars	Benjamin	43	real $800, personal $100	Forgeman	M	M	PA	
M	Mars	Lenah	36			F	M	PA	
M	Mars	Elizabeth	18		Domestic	F	M	PA	
M	Mars	Rachel	3			F	M	PA	
M	Mars	Aaron	2			M	M	PA	
B	Mathews	Anna	38			F	M	MD	Illiterate
B	Mathews	Samuel	19			M	M	MD	Attended school.
B	Mathews	Nelson	18			M	M	PA	Attended school.
B	Mathews	Nancy	15			F	M	PA	
B	Mathews	Martha	13			F	M	PA	Attended school.
B	Mathews	William H.	10			M	M	PA	Attended school.
B	Mathews	Edward	8			M	M	PA	Attended school.
B	Mathews	Rebecca	5			F	M	PA	Attended school.
B	Mathews	Thomas	4			M	M	PA	
B	Mathews	Margaret	1			F	M	PA	
M	Mathews	Samuel	20		Farm laborer	M	B	PA	Listed as living w/Mary & Cyrus Griest.

TWP M/B	LAST NAME	FIRST NAME	AGE	VALUE OF PROPERTY	OCCUPATION	GENDER M/F	COLOR B/C/M	BIRTH-PLACE	COMMENTS
1860 continued		*Total 76*							
M	Mathews	Nelson	18		Farm laborer	M	B	PA	Listed as living w/Hiram Griest, farmer. Attended school.
B	Mathews	Edward	54	real $800, personal $250	Farmer	M	M	MD	Illiterate. N.B.: Annie, Edward, and first child born in MD, remainder PA.
M	Mays	Sarah	11			F	M	PA	Lived w/Henry Weigle, farmer. Attended school.
M	Michaels	Susan	56	personal $25		F	B	PA	
M	Michaels	Sarah	30		Domestic	F	B	PA	
M	Michaels	Mary	27		Domestic	F	B	PA	
M	Michaels	Joseph	26		Day laborer	M	B	PA	
B	Plowden	Catharine	18		Domestics	F	B	PA	Lived w/John Keiter, coachmaker born in Bavaria.
B	Plowden	Ammon	16		Farm laborer	M	B	PA	Listed as living w/Hiram Griest, farmer. Attended school.
B	Rayhaus	Jane	14		Helper	F	B	PA	Lived w/Joseph Smith, physician.
B	Sanders	Jo??	35		Day laborer	M	B	PA	
B	Sanders	Jane	25	personal $300		F	B	PA	
B	Sanders	Richard	2			M	B	PA	
B	Sanders	James	1			M	B	PA	
M	Sanders	James	70	real $200, personal $110		M	B	PA	Blind
M	Sanders	Violet	65			F	B	PA	Illiterate
B	Smith	Charles W.	10			M	M	PA	
B	Smith	Charles	47	personal $100	Waiter	M	B	PA	
B	Smith	Mary	47		Farmhand	F	B	PA	
B	Smith	Sarah	2			F	M	PA	
M	Stephens	John	75	real $50, personal $40		M	B	PA	
M	Stephens	Lydia	70			F	B	PA	
M	Stephens	Louisa	20		Domestic	F	B	PA	
M	Walker	Martha	6			F	M	PA	Lived w/Susan Michaels.
M	Woods	John	35	real $200, personal $100	Day laborer	M	M	PA	
M	Woods	Rachel	28			F	M	PA	
M	Woods	Elizabeth	10			F	M	PA	
M	Woods	Wesley	8			M	M	PA	
M	Woods	Ann	2			M	M	PA	Gender says M but probably F.

TWP M/B	LAST NAME	FIRST NAME	AGE	VALUE OF PROPERTY	OCCUPATION	GENDER M/F	COLOR B/C/M	BIRTH-PLACE	COMMENTS
1870	Total 53								
M	Arnold	Charles	24		Farm laborer	M	B	GA	Lived w/Jacob Roustzohn family; illiterate.
M	Buckmaster	Elizabeth	60		Keeping house	F	B	PA	Couldn't write.
M	Butler	Peter	53	real $4000, personal $500	Works in Forge	M	B	MD	All Butler children went to school within the year.
M	Butler	Harriet	48		Keeping home	F	M	PA	
M	Butler	Henry	15		Farm laborer	M	M	PA	
M	Butler	Harriet	14			F	M	PA	
M	Butler	Thomas	11			M	M	PA	
M	Butler	Amanda	8			F	M	PA	
M	Coby?	Thomas	62	real $300, personal $100	Farm laborer	M	M	MD	Illiterate
M	Coby?	Esther	65		Keeping house	F	M	PA	Illiterate
M	Coleman	Nathan	85	real $400	Basket maker	M	B	WV	
M	Coleman	Nancy	59		Keeping house	F	B	PA	Couldn't write.
M	Coleman	Samuel	9			M	B	PA	Attended school within the year.
B	Draden	George	22		Farm laborer	M	B	PA	Lived w/John Steinour.
M	Gorden	Susan	16		Domestic servant	F	B	PA	Attended school within the year. Lived w/William Morrison family, property 11,000.
B	Harr	John	60	real $1000, personal $400	Farmer	M	B	PA	Illiterate
M	Hill	Charles	44		Farm laborer	M	B	MD	Couldn't write.
M	Hill	Harriet	33		Keeping house	F	B	MD	Couldn't write.
M	Jones	Amon	70	real $300	Fence maker	M	B	MD	Illiterate
M	Jones	Eliza	33		Keeping house	F	B	MD	Illiterate
M	Lewis	John	13		Day laborer	M	M	PA	Lived w/Henry Scott family. Attended school within the year.
M	Mars(on)	Benjamin	53	real $1000, personal $450	Farmer	M	M	MD	
M	Mars(on)	Hanah	43		Keeping house	F	M	PA	
M	Mars(on)	Susan	23			F	M	PA	
M	Mars(on)	Rachel	13			F	M	PA	The four children here and below attended school.
M	Mars(on)	Aaron	11			M	M	PA	
M	Mars(on)	Anna	9			F	M	PA	Illiterate
M	Mars(on)	Ada	6			F	M	PA	

43

TWP M/B	LAST NAME	FIRST NAME	AGE	VALUE OF PROPERTY	OCCUPATION	GENDER M/F	COLOR B/C/M	BIRTH-PLACE	COMMENTS
1870 continued	*Total 53*								
M	Butler	Thomas	11			M	M	PA	
M	Butler	Amanda	8			F	M	PA	
M	Coby?	Thomas	62	real $300, personal $100	Farm laborer	M	M	MD	Illiterate
M	Coby?	Esther	65		Keeping house	F	M	PA	Illiterate
M	Coleman	Nathan	85	real $400	Basket maker	M	B	WV	
M	Coleman	Nancy	59		Keeping house	F	B	PA	Couldn't write.
M	Coleman	Samuel	9			M	B	PA	Attended school within the year.
B	Draden	George	22		Farm laborer	M	B	PA	Lived w/John Steinour.
M	Gorden	Susan	16		Domestic servant	F	B	PA	Attended school within the year. Lived w/William Morrison family, property 11,000.
B	Harr	John	60	real $1000, personal $400	Farmer	M	B	PA	Illiterate
M	Hill	Charles	44		Farm laborer	M	B	MD	Couldn't write.
M	Hill	Harriet	33		Keeping house	F	B	MD	Couldn't write.
M	Jones	Amon	70	real $300	Fence maker	M	B	MD	Illiterate
M	Jones	Eliza	33		Keeping house	F	B	MD	Illiterate
M	Lewis	John	13		Day laborer	M	M	PA	Lived w/Henry Scott family. Attended school within the year.
M	Mars(on)	Benjamin	53	real $1000, personal $450	Farmer	M	M	MD	
M	Mars(on)	Hanah	43		Keeping house	F	M	PA	
M	Mars(on)	Susan	23			F	M	PA	
M	Mars(on)	Rachel	13			F	M	PA	The four children here and below attended school.
M	Mars(on)	Aaron	11			M	M	PA	
M	Mars(on)	Anna	9			F	M	PA	
M	Mars(on)	Ada	6			F	M	PA	
M	Mars(on)	Laura	4			F	M	PA	
M	Mathews	Samuel	29	personal $350	Farmer	M	M	PA	Illiterate
M	Mathews	Elizabeth	26		Keeping house	F	M	PA	
M	Mathews	Morris	3			M	M	PA	
M	Mathews	Mary	1			F	M	PA	
M	Mathews	William	2?	personal $150	Farmer	M	M	PA	

TWP M/B	LAST NAME	FIRST NAME	AGE	VALUE OF PROPERTY	OCCUPATION	GENDER M/F	COLOR B/C/M	BIRTH-PLACE	COMMENTS
1870 continued		*Total 53*							
M	Mathews	Mary	19		Keeping house	F	M	MD	Couldn't write.
M	Mathews	Joseph	9			M	W	PA	Attended school within the year.
M	Michael	Susan	71		Keeping house	F	B	PA	Illiterate
M	Michael	Joseph	36		Farm laborer	M	B	PA	
M	Michael	Sarah	43	real $150		F	B	PA	Couldn't write.
M	Reed	Samuel	27		Farmer	M	B	PA	
M	Reed	Nancy	24		Keeping house	F	B	PA	
M	Scott	Henry	27	personal $150	Works in Forge	M	B	PA	
M	Scott	Susan	23		Keeping house	F	M	PA	
M	Scott	Elmore	6			M	M	PA	
M	Scott	Estella	3			F	M	PA	
M	Smith	Daniel D	24		Farm laborer	M	B	PA	
M	Smith	Elizabeth	20		Keeping house	F	B	PA	Illiterate
M	Smith	Samuel	1			M	B	PA	
M	William	Elizabeth	16			F	B	PA	
M	Woods	John	42	real $800, personal $200	Farm laborer	M	M	PA	Couldn't write.
M	Woods	Wesley	18		Farm laborer	M	M	PA	Attended school within the year.
M	Woods	Alice	3			F	M	PA	
M	Woods	Wilson	b.rn May 1870		M	M	PA		
1880		*Total 51*							
B	Ayers	Thomas	23			M	B		
M	Brown	Minnie	20			F	B		
M	Brown	Rachel	5 mo			F	B		
M	Brown	William	26			M	B		
B	Butler	Jessie	81			M	B		
M	Butler	Peter	57			M	B		
M	Butler	Harriet	57			F	B		
M	Butler	Daniel	31			M	B		
M	Butler	Jennie	7			F	B		

TWP M/B	LAST NAME	FIRST NAME	AGE	VALUE OF PROPERTY	OCCUPATION	GENDER M/F	COLOR B/C/M	BIRTH-PLACE	COMMENTS
1880 continued		Total 51							
M	Butler	John	4			M	B		
M	Butler	Lydia	1			F	B		
M	Butler	Martha	25			F	B		
M	Butler	Thomas	21			M	B		
M	Harris	Harry	15			M	B		
M	Harris	Lincoln	14			M	B		
M	Mares	Benjamin	63			M	B		
M	Mares	Ida	17			F	B		
M	Mares	Lach	52			F	B		
B	Mathew	Anna	62			M	B		
B	Mathew	Josiah	20			F	B		
B	Mathew	Martha	23			F	B		
B	Mathew	Ruth	16			F	B		
M	Mathews	William	31			M	B		
M	Mathews	George	5			F	B		
M	Mathews	Mary	29			F	B		
M	Mathews	Nettie	7			F	B		
M	Mathews	Lewis	10			M	B		
M	Naylor	Bertha	5 mo			F	B		
M	Naylor	Harrison	22			M	B		
M	Naylor	Thomas	20			M	B		
M	Parker	Catharin	34			F	B		Eli Parker, a 45-year-old white man, may have been Catharin's husband.
M	Parker	Elmer	3			M	B		
M	Parker	Harry	9			M	B		
M	Parker	Mary	12			F	B		
M	Reed	Samuel	37			M	B		
M	Reed	Nancy	33			F	B		
B	Scott	Carrie	6			F	B		
B	Scott	Charles	10			M	B		

TWP M/B	LAST NAME	FIRST NAME	AGE	VALUE OF PROPERTY	OCCUPATION	GENDER M/F	COLOR B/C/M	BIRTH-PLACE	COMMENTS
1880 continued		*Total 51*							
B	Scott	Emma	6 mo			F	B		
B	Scott	Ida	2			F	B		Two more Scotts (Harry age 5, Lizzie, age 29) are listed but both are shown as white.
B	Scott	Martha	34			F	B		
B	Scott	Mary	5			F	B		
B	Scott	William	11			M	B		
M	Woods	Alice	14			F	B		
M	Woods	?	6/12..			F	B		
M	Woods	Della	8			F	B		
M	Woods	Emily	2			F	B		
M	Woods	John	50			M	B		
M	Woods	Margaret	21			F	B		
M	Woods	Rachel	48			F	B		
M	Woods	Wesley	28			M	B		
1900		*Total 5*							
B	Chris	Francis	18			M	B	MD	
M	Hill	Charley	69			M	B		
M	Hill	Anna H.	61			F	B		
B	Robinson	Henry	45			M	B	MD	Farmer
B	Robinson	Mart	42			F	B		
1910		*Total 1*							
M		Clara	18		Servant	F	M	MD	

Compiled by author

47

Appendix II

Warrants for slave removals issued in Adams County

The following information is from microfilm records at the Adams County Courthouse.

Be it remembered that on the fourteenth day of June eighteen hundred and twenty-eight Singleton Burgee, of Frederick County in the state of Maryland brought before the subscriber one of the judges of the court of Common Pleas for said county a dark mulatto man called James Campbell, 5 ft 6 in high, 30 years old, has a scar on his hand and acknowledged himself to be the slave of said Burgess, to whom an order was granted on the same day for his removal according to law. Given my hand and seal this 16th day of June 1828. *M McClean*

Be it remembered that on the fourteenth day of October Eighteen hundred and twenty eight, William Clagett of Prince George County in the state of Maryland brought before the subscriber one of the Judges of the Court of Common Please for said County by virtue of a warrant issued by Justice Baugher. A Negro man called Henry, eighteen years of age, five feel high-dark colour, satisfactory evidence being had, that said Henry owed service to the said Mr. Clagett in a Warrant for removal was granted according to law. Given under my hand . . .

Be it remembered that on this thirteenth day of June A. D. 1828 Benjamin Beal, the legally authorized Agent of Roger Johnston of Frederick County Maryland, brought before me one of the Judges of the Court of Common Pleas for said County, Negro Isaac Thomas who says he is the property of said Johnston. He is fifty years of age 5 feet 8 inched high dark complexion, had a wart on one side of his face. I have therefore granted a warrant of removal to the said Benjamin Beals according to law. Given under my hand . . .

Twenty seventh day of May Eighteen hundred and twenty eight, Doc. Frederick Dorsey of Washington County in the state of Maryland, obtained from the subscriber one of the Judges of the Court of Common Pleas, for said county a warrant of removal for his Negro slave Jonas Poyer, light-colored stout male, about five feet ten inches in height, supposed to be twenty five years of age. Given under my hand and seal this fifth day of June eighteen hundred and twenty eight. *M McClean*

Whereas Walter C. Winston of Culpepper County in the state of Virginia hath this day in pursuance of a warrant granted by the subscriber, one of the Judges of the Court of Common Pleas for said County-brought before me Negro Edmund, who acknowledged he was the slave of said Winston. He is dark color, five feet five inches high between twenty five and thirty years of age-bends forward in walking, has a large scar on the inside of his right wrist. A warrant for his removal was therefore granted to said owner conformably to the act of assembly in such case made and provided. Given under my hand and seal this ? day of May 1829.

Be it remembered that on this thirteenth day of June eighteen hundred and twenty-eight William Kingsbury, the properly authorized agent of Benjamin Murdock of Frederick County Maryland, brought before me one of the Judges of the Court of Common Pleas for the county, Negro Caleb who says he is the slave of said Murdock-forty years of age, 5 ft 8 or 9 inches high, dark yellow complexion. I have granted a warrant of removal to the said Wm. Kingsbury according to law.

Granted a warrant to Wm. P. Mills of Baltimore County Maryland for the removal of Negro Mary about 18 or 19 years old, middle stature and a lively gait. She acknowledged the ownership of said Mills. Given my hand and seal this day. *M McClean*

I hereby certify that on the 2nd day of June 1830 agreeably to the provision of an act for the recovery of Fugitive Slaves I have Granted a Warrant for the removal of a Mulatto Man who acknowledged himself to be the slave of Michael Blessing of Frederick County Maryland to whom the warrant was granted. He is 27 years of age, about 5 feet 3 inches high stout make said Blessing giving evidence . . . with the acknowledgement of said slave.

Appeared before me the subscriber one of the judges of the court of Common Pleas for said county Elisha Howard of Carroll man or Frederick county state of Maryland who on his solumn oath doth say that he believes his negro man Garret whom he holds to labour in said state has escaped into Pennsylvania and that he has reason to suspect that he is now in the hands of said County of Adams. And thus identifies this person twenty five years of age stout make, dark mulatto and that he absconded about the first of Nov. last. Sworn and subscribed before me this 10th day of March 1827. *Elisha Howard*

State of Negro Jim & Ephraim Valentine. Warrant to ask constable to apprehend a pair of slaves on the ask of Nimrod Owings of the county of Frederick in the state of Maryland, who is the owner of the said slaves. I certify that the above is a copy of the record in the above case as entered in my docket, which my hand eight seal at Gettysburg the 4th day of June 1834. *Lampkin L. King*

On application of George Shiess of Washington County in the state of Maryland (near Lightersburg) on evidence of his Oath Warrant granted by Amos Maginly Esq. a Justice of the Peace to Harry Lucket (a man of color) whom he claims as a slave. Said Harry is described to be about twenty two years of age five feet four or six inches high, stutters when spoken to, has a down look hat on, when went away a drab coat pantaloons and vest of . . . Witness my hand the 19th day of December 1827 agreeably to act of Assembly paper March 25, 1827. *A. Maginly*

Whereas John Jsh of London County Virginia, the regularly authorized agent of Sarah Ellsy of the County and state aforesaid, hath this day procured from the subscriber, one of the Judges of the court of Common Pleas for said County, a warrant for the removal of Negro George, who acknowledges himself to be the slave of the said Sarah Ellsey. He is black, about 5 feet 8 in high, slim make, between the ages of 20 & 26 years, Given my hand and seal this 12th day of June 1828. *M McClean*

The following "calendar of prisoners" was found among the removal warrants:

To the honorable Judges of the Court of Common Pleas for Adams County—A calendar of the Prisoners now in confirmation in Publick Jail. Charles Valentine, a runaway affirmative from Wm. Willing Baltimore. Rachel, a Black Girl on suspicion of having mixed arsnech with sugar with intent to take away the life of Elizabeth Dunwoody, her late mistress. August 15, 1808

Transcribed by the author

Appendix III

Kitty Payne's plight

During 1845 and 1846 citizens of Adams County read numerous newspaper accounts of the kidnapping of Kitty Payne and her children, of the kidnappers' trial in Pennsylvania, and of Payne's battle for freedom in Virginia. The party who instigated prosecution of Payne's kidnappers was The Society of Friends.[171]

Kitty Payne's story began in Rappahannock County Virginia. Deciding after her husband's death to free their slaves, the widow Mary Maddox "manumitted" Kitty Payne and her three children, and two other men, James and Ben. She brought them across the Mason-Dixon Line to Adams County and lived with them for nine months, during which time she sought out a Justice of the Peace where she filed a second set of manumission papers. Then Mrs. Maddox returned to Virginia.

Samuel Maddox, a nephew of Mary Maddox, was to inherit the Maddox estate at Mary's death, and he considered his uncle's slaves to be his rightful property. Under cover of darkness, Samuel Maddox and four men broke into Kitty's home near Bendersville, bound and gagged her and the children, loaded them into a wagon, and took them back to Virginia and into slavery once again. Someone witnessed the kidnapping and contacted the authorities. The five kidnappers were named and a trial was held in Gettysburg, although the kidnappers were not present. They were found guilty, but because they were not in custody, no justice could be served. The Adams County sheriff issued written requests to Rappahannock County, Virginia, for the return of the guilty men, but to no avail.

Later, however, one of the kidnappers, a professional slave catcher named Thomas Finnegan, was recognized in Gettysburg heading north toward Bendersville. He was probably returning to kidnap James and Ben, the two men that Mary Maddox had freed along

---

17. "Court Doings, Court of Quarter Sessions—August Term," *Star and Republican Banner* (Gettysburg, PA), August 28, 1846.

with Kitty. Outraged, a few Gettysburg citizens followed him while others summoned the sheriff. Finnegan turned tail and headed south. After getting an arrest warrant, Sheriff Schriver set off in hot pursuit atop his horse, Old Ben, and captured the criminal who, in turned out, was heavily armed.

Finnegan was brought to the county jail where an angry mob had gathered to "cage the bird".[18] He was later sentenced to five years of hard labor and solitary confinement. Though all five kidnappers were found guilty and Finnegan punished, Kitty Payne lost her fight for freedom in the Virginia courts.

From the records it appears that Kitty Payne had a relationship with the Friends. Her three children were found to be living in Adams County, in three different townships, according to the 1850 census. Two were with the Friends. Her daughter Mary was living on the Quaker farm owned by John Wright in the Quaker Valley.[19] Arthur Pain, age nine, was living on the Quaker farm owned by John Tudor in Latimore Township.[20] Eliza Pain, aged twelve, was living on the Alexander Camel (identified on a later document as "Campbell") farm in Straban Township.[21]

Kitty later regained her freedom and returned to Gettysburg where she became the second wife of Abraham Brian. She was the mother of a daughter, Francis. Kitty died in August 1850 and is buried in Gettysburg's Lincoln Cemetery. Interestingly, Abraham Brian's farm was located near the "copse of trees" that came to symbolize the High Water Mark of the Confederacy, and a monument was later erected on his land.

According to the "Bill of Costs" compiled by the Commonwealth at the time of Kitty's 1846 kidnapping trial, witnesses who gave depositions included:

---

18. "Important Arrest: Finnegan, the Kidnapper, in JAIL!!" *Star and Banner* (Gettysburg, PA), May 26, 1846.
19. Menallen Township Census Records, 1850 (Gettysburg, PA: Adams County Courthouse).
20. Latimore Township Census Records, 1850 (Gettysburg, PA: Adams County Courthouse).
21. Straban Township Census Records, 1850 (Gettysburg, PA: Adams County Courthouse).

James Wilson, Charles Moyer, Amon Jones, Rachael Jones, Jane Roberts, John Rice, Aaron Cox, George Bender, Eliza Hewitt, James Green, Jacob Keckler, Cyrus Griest, George McClelland, Christian Musser, Isaac Wireman, Jese Cook, William Wright, H. E. Donaldson, Henry Martin, Christian Staub.

Of these 20 witnesses, at least five—Cyrus Griest, Jessie Cook, William Wright, Eliza Hewitt, and Isaac Wireman—were Menallen Friends. Another four witnesses—Amon and Rachel Jones, Jane Roberts, and James Green—were African Americans listed in Butler and Menallen Township census records. Court records also list how far each witness had to come to get to the courthouse in Gettysburg, and these distances are consistent with travel from the area in and around Quaker Valley, Yellow Hill, and Bendersville.

The Kitty Payne affair is one well-documented case of Adams County abolitionist activity from which is it apparent the Quakers and African Americans were working together. There may have been others.

Compiled by the author

Newspaper accounts of the church at Yellow Hill

Rev. Charles Maddix named to serve Gettysburg and Yellow Hill by A. M. E. Zion Conference. (*Star and Sentinel*, June 16, 1871)

Wood's Meeting. A woods meeting will be held at Fairmount church (Yellow Hill) in John Crum's woods, one mile northwest of Middletown, commencing August 3rd and to continue over the 4th. Rev. S. Hammond will conduct the services, assisted by ministers from abroad. Refreshments on the ground. (*Star and Sentinel*, July 23, 1878)

Bush Meeting. The Fairmount M. E. Church will hold a bush meeting near Middletown, beginning July 26, 1879. The Revs. N. A. Carrol and J. N. Riddick, both of Baltimore, are expected to be with us. We cordially invite the people of your town and vicinity to attend. (*Star and Sentinel*, July 17, 1879)

Butler Items. A fine shower on Sunday evening made quite a scatterment of the people who were attending a Bush meeting, held by the colored folks in the pine grove of Frank Osborn, near Flora Dale. (*Star and Sentinel*, September 1, 1885)

The A. M. E. Church at Fairmount will hold an entertainment on the evening of Feb. 12, to consist of singing, dialogues, & c., the proceeds to be devoted to church interests. (*Star and Sentinel*, January 20, 1886)

There will be a Day's Meeting at Fairmount M. E. Church, Yellow Hill, Sunday, Oct. 4th. (*Star and Sentinel*, September 29, 1886)

Memorial Services were held at Fairmount church, two miles above Biglerville, by colored Comrads. W. M. Biggs was master of ceremonies and addresses delivered by N. F. Matthews and S. S. Stanton. Mrs. Harriet Butler offered prayer and the exercises were interspersed with singing. (*Gettysburg Compiler*, June 5, 1894)

Remains Reinterred. The remains of Edward Matthews, who died in 1876 and was interred at Fairmount were last week brought to Gettysburg and reinterred beside his wife in the colored graveyard, South Washington Street. (*Star and Sentinel*, May 20, 1903)

County Firemen in Session. Good Parade and Big Day in
Biglerville on July 4th. The Adams County Firemen's Association at their quarterly meeting in Thomas Brothers' Hall on
July 4th elected George Felix, of McSherrystown, as a county
representative to the State Firemen's Association in Reading in
October. . . . The Biglerville meeting was the occasion of a
fireman's parade, baseball game, festival, and dance. . . . The
order of the parade was as follows: The East Berlin Company
with its band, led the line of march. Then followed by Mt.
Rock Centennial Company: McSherrystown, with its band; the
Gettysburg Company with the new La France engine, and the
Gettysburg Band; the Biglerville firemen and their apparatus in
line and a band accompanied their ranks; Yellowhill Fire
Company, composed of colored residents of Yellowhill,
brought up the rear of the line. (*Gettysburg Compiler,* July 14,
1923)

Appendix V

Friends of the Quaker Valley

Records in the Adams County Courthouse and the Friends Meetinghouse indicate that the Friends and the community on Yellow Hill interacted and enjoyed cordial, cooperative relations. This existence of documents on which Friends' names are commingled with African American names bear this out.

V.1 The Friends have been meeting at this location since the 1830s. This meetinghouse was built in the 1880s and has changed little since that time. Cyrus Griest and many other Friends are buried in the cemetery in back.

The Friends were scrupulous recordkeepers; their meetings were minuted, and the minutes were later bound into books. These volumes contain a wealth of information about their membership and activities, including the names of members, and dates of marriages, births, and deaths. Margaret B. Walmer has published many of these minutes. By comparing the information about the African Americans found in census records with the names of the Friends, one can get to know the people who lived on Yellow Hill and in the Quaker Valley in the 1800s.

The Menallen Meeting is still active today. A visit to their well-maintained cemetery reveals the names of many Friends who once worshipped there.

V.2 Menallen Friends in 1923 at Caledonia for the dedication of the Lincoln Highway: (standing) Edith Peters Coates, Alice Black, Ethel Wright, Lola Griest, Beulah Harris, Anna Black, Wallace Peters, Muriel Tyson Parsons, Edna Tyson, Esther Prickett Stubbs, Richard Walton, Lucille Watson; (seated) Arthur Cook, Arthur Griest, William C. Tyson, Frederick C. Griest.

The Menallen Friends began meeting in 1780 at their first meetinghouse on the Centre Mills Road, just off Route 234 between Biglerville and Heidlersburg. If you are traveling east, the cemetery is visible on the left just past the intersection of the Centre Mills Road and Route 234. Many of the Friends who came to Menallen had been members of the Huntingdon

V.3 & V.4 *Charles and Maria Tyson*

V.5 *Loma Vista ("View of the Hills") was once owned by Charles and Maria Tyson. The rail of the now-demolished Guernsey Bridge is visible in the foreground.*

Meeting near York Springs, which had been part of the westward movement of York County's Warrington and Redland Meetings.

Many Griests were living in the Quaker Valley prior to the Civil War having come there from farther east in York County. Charles Tyson and his brother Philip came to Adams County from Philadelphia just before the Civil War to open a photography studio. Charles was a member of the Religious Society of Friends. In those days Friends who did not marry other Friends risked being dismissed from the the Society, so Charles Tyson headed north to the Quaker Valley to find a bride. There he met and married Maria, daughter of Cyrus Griest. Following their wedding in spring 1863—just a few weeks before the start of the Battle of Gettysburg—Charles and Maria moved into a house on Chambersburg Street in Gettysburg. They survived the three-day battle, and Charles photographed the battlefield, the soldiers, and President Lincoln when he later visited Gettysburg. Tiring of photography, Charles became interested in the Griest's farming businesses, so the Tysons returned to Maria's roots in the Quaker Valley where they had three sons and one daughter.

During the 1870s the Tysons operated Mapleton Seminary. In the early 1900s two Tyson sons formed Tyson Brothers, Inc., and expanded Adams County's fruit-growing industry. Bertha Tyson's 1919 diary mentions son Chester traveling by train across the United States and to State College (PA), where he lobbied for more fruit research. Establishment of the Penn State Fruit Research Laboratory near Yellow Hill resulted in large part from Chester Tyson's efforts. Work

V.6 This stately home was once Mapleton Seminary (1871). At another time it housed offices of Charles Tyson's Susquehanna Fertilizer Company, owned by Charles Tyson.

V.7 This beautiful Victorian-era structure, Hill House, sits in the Quaker Valley between Biglerville and Bendersville. It is still owned by the great granddaughter of its builder, Chester Tyson, son of Maria and Charles Tyson. Chester and his wife, Bertha, raised more than 10 children here.

carried on there today informs fruit growers about more effective farming methods that result in higher crop yields.

During the nineteenth and early twentieth centuries, the Friends of Menallen contributed in many ways to the prosperity and advancement of the area known today as the Quaker Valley, leaving a legacy in which we all share.

Appendix VI

A Quaker general?

The fact that William Wierman Wright served in the Civil War is interesting in itself, since the Friends were usually pacifists and did not take part in armed conflict. But Wright apparently chose to serve because of his strong feelings about slavery, and wished to use his skills to aid the abolitionist cause. The following information is from Chattanooga, Tennessee, and dated February 19, 1864.

Major General George H. Thomas, Commanding Department of the Cumberland is hereby authorized to raise a Regiment of Infantry of African Descent from such men as may now be disposed at Chattanooga, or who may hereafter come within the lines. The Regiment will be composed of all classes of Colored men.

William W. Wright, Chief Engineer, United States Military Rail Road, Division of the Mississippi, is hereby appointed Colonel of the Regiment authorized above.

Colonel W. W. Wright will be reported on detached service in order that he may carryout the specific duties assigned him by the War Department as Chief Engineer of the U. S. Military Rail Roads.

Wright's signature appears on this document.

Wright served as chief engineer to General Sherman during the infamous March to the Sea. In his memoirs, Sherman praised Wright, who was breveted for his service.

General William Wierman Wright is buried next to his abolitionist parents, William and Phebe, in the cemetery of the Huntingdon Meeting.

Bibliography

Adams County Courthouse, Gettysburg, PA. Latimore Township Census Records, 1850.

Adams County Courthouse, Gettysburg, PA. Menallen Township Census Records, 1850.

Adams County Courthouse, Gettysburg, PA. Quarter Session Records, 1846. Microfilm.

Adams County Courthouse, Gettysburg, PA. Straban Township Census Records, 1850.

Adams County Courthouse, Gettysburg, PA. Will of Edward Mathews, 1874. File 4968.

Alosi, John. *Shadow of Freedom: Slavery in Post-Revolutionary Cumberland County, 1780–1810*. Shippensburg, PA: Shippensburg University Press, 1994.

Blockson, Charles. *African Americans in Pennsylvania, Above Ground and Underground: An Illustrated Guide*. Harrisburg, PA: Sietz and Sietz, 2001.

Bloom, Robert L. *A History of Adams County, Pennsylvania, 1700– 1900*. Gettysburg, PA: Adams County Historical Society, c1992.

Bunie, Andrew. *Robert L. Vann of the* Pittsburgh Courier: *Politics and Black Journalism*. Pittsburgh, PA: University of Pittsburgh Press, 1974.

Myers, Betty Dorsey. *Segregation in Death: Gettysburg's Lincoln Cemetery*. Gettysburg, PA: Lincoln Cemetery Project.

Neely, George M., Jr. "The Anti-Slavery Movement and Underground Railroad Activity in Adams County" (Gettysburg College thesis, 1930). Gettysburg, PA: Adams County Historical Society.

Walmer, Margaret B. *Menallen Minutes, Marriages and Miscellany*. Bowie, MD: Heritage Books, Inc., 1922.

Wilson, William B. *Diary of William B. Wilson, 1829–1871*, 3 vol. Harrisburg, PA: State Library of Pennsylvania.

Suggested Resources

http://www.ancestry.com

Bolin, Larry C. *Slaveholders and Slaves of Adams County*. Gettysburg, PA: Adams County Historical Society, 2003.

Botkin, B. A., ed. *Lay My Burden Down: A Folk History of Slavery.* University of Chicago Press, 1945.

Frassanito, William. *Early Photography at Gettysburg*. Gettysburg, PA: Thomas Publications, 1995.

http://www.afrolumens.org

http://www.heritagequest.com

McPherson, James M. *The Negro's Civil War*. New York: Pantheon Books, 1965.

http://www.newspaperarchives.com

Paradis, James. *Strike the Blow for Freedom*. Shippensburg, PA: White Mane Books, 1998.

Pennington, James W. C. *The Fugitive Blacksmith*. Westport, CN: Negro Universities Press, 1850. Reprinted 1971.

Siebert, Wilber H. *Underground Railroad, From Slavery to Freedom*. New York: The MacMillan Company, 1898.

Still, William J. *The Underground Railroad*. New York: Arno Press, 1968. Reprint of 1872 edition.

Switala, William J. *The Underground Railroad in Pennsylvania.* Mechanicsburg, PA: Stackpole Books, 2001.

Trudeau, Noah Andre. *Like Men of War: The Black Troops of 1862–1865*. Boston: Little Brown, 1998.

Afterword

If you can help us preserve the cemetery at Yellow Hill, please send your donation to the Historic Preservation Society of Gettysburg/ Adams County (HPSGAC), P. O. Box 4611, Gettysburg, PA 17325.

HPSGAC can be reached by calling (717) 334-5185. Leave a message and someone will get back to you. This organization is not to be confused with the Adams County Historical Society, where much of the research was obtained.

You can find out more about the Yellow Hill preservation effort by contacting the author at For the Cause Productions located at 2699 Heidlersburg Road in Gettysburg, PA 17325, (717) 528-8553. To learn more about local history and For the Cause Productions, visit www.gettysburghistories.com.

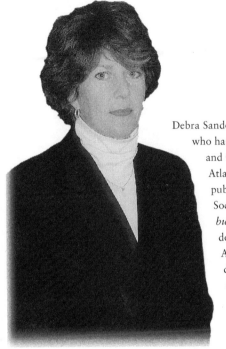

Debra Sandoe McCauslin is an avid local historian who has made presentations to historical societies and Civil War roundtables throughout the mid-Atlantic area. Several of her articles have been published by the Adams County Historical Society, the *Gettysburg Times,* and *Gettysburg Experience* magazine. She produced the documentary *Adams County USA* for the Adams County Historical Society. A descendant of George Washington Sandoe, first to fall at the Battle of Gettysburg, Debra provided research for a story of his life written by T. W. Burger (*Civil War Times,* August 2000).

Made in the USA
Middletown, DE
27 February 2023

25540177R00047